Helping the Community

What Do DOCTORS Do?

Amy B. Rogers

PowerKiDS press™

New York

Published in 2016 by The Rosen Publishing Group, Inc.
29 East 21st Street, New York, NY 10010

First Edition

Editor: Katie Kawa
Book Design: Katelyn Heinle

Photo Credits: Cover (doctor), p. 1 william casey/Shutterstock.com; cover (hands) bymandesigns/Shutterstock.com; series back cover Zffoto/Shutterstock.com; p. 5 Jovan Mandic/Shutterstock.com; p. 6 Ilike/Shutterstock.com; p. 9 Levent Konuk/Shutterstock.com; pp. 10, 24 (coat) michaeljung/Shutterstock.com; pp. 13, 24 (nurse) Konstantin Chagin/Shutterstock.com; p. 14 LWA/The Image Bank/Getty Images; p. 17 Odua Images/ Shutterstock.com; p. 18 wavebreakmedia/Shutterstock.com; pp. 21, 24 (medicine) Miodrag Gajic/E+/ Getty Images; p. 22 racorn/Shutterstock.com.

Library of Congress Cataloging-in-Publication Data

Rogers, Amy B.
 What do doctors do? / Amy B. Rogers.
     pages cm. — (Helping the community)
Includes bibliographical references and index.
ISBN 978-1-4994-0617-7 (pbk.)
ISBN 978-1-4994-0621-4 (6 pack)
ISBN 978-1-4994-0623-8 (library binding)
1. Physicians—Juvenile literature. 2. Medical care—Juvenile literature. I. Title.
R690.R589 2015
610—dc23
                              2015000443

Manufactured in the United States of America

CPSIA Compliance Information: Batch #WS15PK: For Further Information contact Rosen Publishing, New York, New York at 1-800-237-9932

CONTENTS

Doctors help you when you are sick.

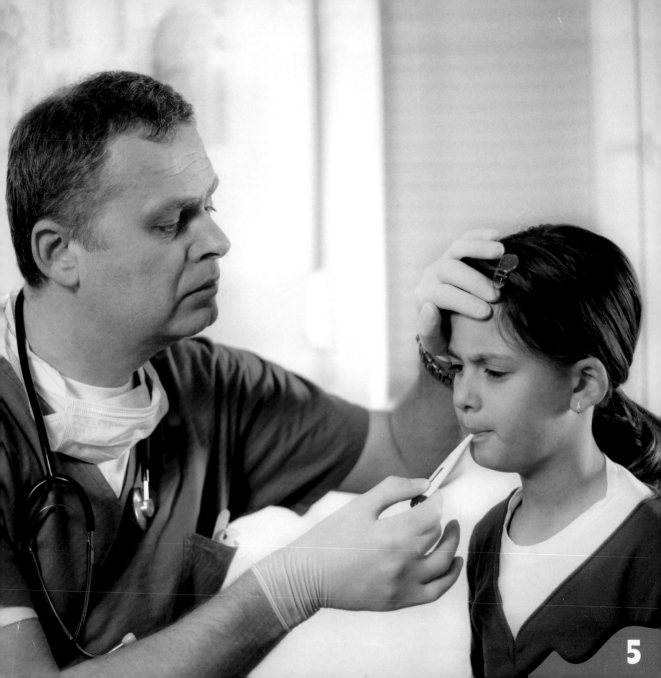

They also help you stay healthy.

Some doctors are just for kids!

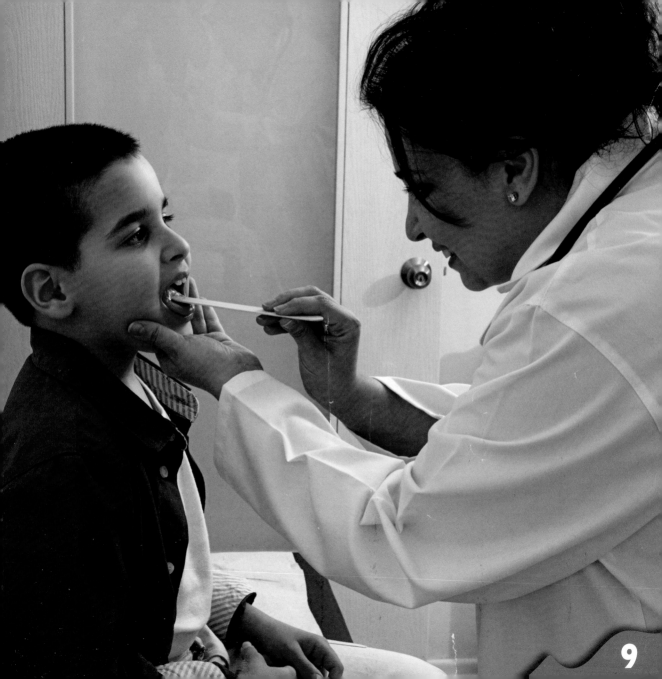

Many doctors wear white **coats**.

Doctors have helpers.
They are called **nurses**.

A doctor sees how tall you are.

A doctor listens to your heart.

A doctor looks at your ears, nose, and throat.

If you are sick, a doctor can give you **medicine**. People take medicine to feel better.

Would you like to be a doctor when you grow up?

WORDS TO KNOW

coat

medicine

nurse

INDEX

WEBSITES

Due to the changing nature of Internet links, PowerKids Press has developed an online list of websites related to the subject of this book. This site is updated regularly. Please use this link to access the list: www.powerkidslinks.com/htc/doc